COMING TO FLOOD

ALSO BY SEBASTIAN MATTHEWS

We Generous (poetry—forthcoming from Red Hen Press)
In My Father's Footsteps (memoir)
Search Party: Collected Poems of William Matthews (co-editor)
The Poetry Blues: Essays & Interviews of William Matthews (co-editor)

COMING TO FLOOD

A Chapbook

Sebastian Matthews

Hollyridge Press
Venice, California

© 2005 Sebastian Matthews
All rights reserved under International and Pan-American Copyright Conventions. Published in the United States by Hollyridge Press.

Hollyridge Press
P.O. Box 2872
Venice, California 90294
www.hollyridgepress.com

Cover and Book Design by Rio Smyth
Author Photo by Alison Climo
Manufactured in the United States of America by Lightning Source

ISBN-13: 978-0-9772298-0-2
ISBN-10: 0-9772298-0-7

Grateful acknowledgment is made to the editors of the publications in which the following poems first appeared:

Asheville Poetry Review: "Coming to Flood"; "We Fall into Shapes and Breathe Deeply"
Atlantic Monthly: "Walking with Walter"
Blue Mesa Review: "Fall"
Fishousepoems.org: "Live at the Village Vanguard"
Forklift: "Love Poem"
Greensboro Review: "What Love Is"
Hanging Loose: "Got Those Cary Grant Blues Again"
New England Review: "Coming into Lexington, Virginia"
Poetry Daily: "Buying Wine" (reprint)
Pool: "Prayer"
Seneca Review: "Round the Bend"
Solo: "Ancestor"; "The Night Before Avery Arrives"
Spinning Jenny: "Wolf with You"
Virginia Quarterly Review: "Buying Wine"

12 11 10 09 08 07 06 05   10 9 8 7 6 5 4 3 2 1

Contents

Love Poem	3
Coming Into Lexington, Virginia	4
Live At The Village Vanguard	6
Ancestor	7
Walking With Walter	8
Coming To Flood	9
Fall	11
Prayer	12
We Generous	13
We Fall Into Shapes And Breathe Deeply	26
Wolf With You	27
Got Those Cary Grant Blues Again	29
Buying Wine	31
Round The Bend	33
The Night Before Avery Arrives	35
What Love Is	36

COMING TO FLOOD

―――――――――――

LOVE POEM

Sitting outside the Little Theatre this morning, listening
      to a lecture on poetic tone—how a poem is a small
skirmish of voices and inflections that play and resolve,
      fight and stand bristling, all inside the poem, all talking,
like yesterday's cocktail party, field and river behind
      in muted counterpoint to the babble of our bodies—
my senses bring my attention to the trees, woken by a shudder
      of breeze (blanket tossed over a bed), each tree
rustling in its own tuning-fork voice, one after the other.
      The way one day in New Hampshire my brother
and I, playing tennis at the end of a long row
      of university courts, got caught in a stampede of rain,
the shower washing over first one court then the next,
      darkening each surface, each empty stage. How
this round of tree song, that passes *into* then *through* me,
      seems now to enter the porous auditorium like a spirit,
touching the poet, who I saw dancing the other night
      in a sufic trance (surrounded by men and women
in couples, dancing, alone, in ragged circles), as he reminds
      us in a microphoned voice that *tone is not feeling
but also all we know about feeling.* Trucks wash by
      in a grimy hallway of rushing wind; the poet cracks
a joke that ripples through the theater, coming back
      in concentric circles of laughter. I imagine I am
ascending a staircase past sunlit rooms and bright panes,
      finally reaching the lost attic of my body, which now,
sitting in this chair, feels like pure Mind, its windows thrown
      open to the poet's words, and to the trees,
which are only broadcasting the arising desire of the mountains.
      (Now that's a line I'll revise.) Soon, he says,
the talk will be over. Soon, I will get up from this chair
      and walk out into the woods. At least in this poem,
at least for you, Beloved, I will keep walking until I've lost
      everything held in my head, and only come back
when you call me, a bell, to the next thing.

COMING INTO LEXINGTON, VIRGINIA

If I were a drifter in town
on foot or off some old Trailways,
free of the lifelines and buoys
that attach to lives like mine,

I'd head for the bar, for
the lonely woman dropping
back a shaft of vodka
for lunch, sword-swallowing

100 proof sadness—her reflection
in the mirror smiling as if
I am an angel who sees her
exactly in all her splendor,

who knows that she'll leave
the man degrading her
by holding her to a treaty
she's not signed. Miraculously,

I have money, clean with pressed
clothes and a rich man's smile,
and I lay down bills for a room
in the town's only respectable

boarding house. And after a long
shower in which I name aloud
in the breezy room all the women
I'd ever slept with, or kissed,

I step out into the streets,
find a fancy bistro with glass tables.
At the bar: my lonely woman,
surrounded by cologned men

busy admiring themselves
in her company, who make room
reluctantly. Before taking her
to our table, I hold forth

on baseball, evoking the great
Sachel Page. Outside, gorgeous
blue night and lights dancing
in car windows. Our meal

as elegant as wedding cake. And
while I'm at it, this sad woman
growing lovely in aloneness, dropped
hands in mine, laughing,

like at a jazz club, drenched in joy,
and the bassist coming off a mountain-
top solo. And, later, I take her
to my room, watch her navigate

the wood steps. There's an old civil war
graveyard across the street
we dream full of former slaves fallen
beside soldiers, confederate and union,

stones worn smooth from the hands
of bored schoolchildren. She undresses
in front of me—dropping her cares, one
piece at a time, onto the unswept floorboards.

LIVE AT THE VILLAGE VANGUARD

Near the end of Bill Evans' "Porgy (I Loves You, Porgy)"
played live at the Village Vanguard and added as an extra track
on *Waltz for Debby* (a session made famous by the death
of the trio's young bassist in a car crash) a woman laughs.
There's been background babble bubbling up the whole set.
You get used to the voices percolating at the songs' fringes,
the clink of glasses and tips of silver on hard plates. Listen
to the recording enough and you almost accept the aural clutter
as another percussive trick the drummer pulls out, like brushes
on a snare. But this woman's voice stands out for its carefree
audacity, how it broadcasts the lovely ascending stair of her happiness.
Evans has just made one of his elegant, casual flights up an octave
and rests on its landing, notes spilling from his left hand
like sunlight, before coming back down into the tune's lush
living-room of a conclusion. The laugh begins softly, subsides,
then lifts up to step over the bass line: five short bursts of pleasure
pushed out of what can only be a long lovely tan throat. Maybe
Evans smiles to himself when he hears it, leaving a little space
between the notes he's cobbled to close the song; maybe
the man she's with leans in, first to still her from the laugh
he's just coaxed from her, then to caress the cascade of her hair
that hangs, lace curtain, in the last vestiges of spotlight stippling the table.

ANCESTOR

Bears have been following me around again.
I saw one the other day, across the road,

snuffling about in his Nature Center pen
up from the polluted river and in sight

of the public golf course. And just tonight
I caught this snippet of National Geographic

on television: a hunter describing how he shot
this young bear; he was crouching somewhere

in the field, face turned from the camera
as he told his story. The man spoke forthrightly

of seeing it coming, of knowing the bear
hadn't spotted him, of making a decision:

if the bear walked into his area, he'd shoot;
if he drifted off, he'd let him go his way.

He came into my view, he said, *and so
raised the gun. Then the bear turned to look*

at me and I shot him. The hunter went on,
his speech slowing, faltering. With distinct sadness

the hunter described the bullet entering the bear,
exploding inside the animal. It wasn't remorse

he choked on: he had done what he had set out
to do. No, I am sure it was recognition I saw

clouding his face. *He went down quick*, he said.
He didn't know what hit him.

WALKING WITH WALTER

—for my father

Walter wants to know how I'm doing
so far, what I think of this and that.
It's a simple gift to be in the beam
of Walter's interest. And there's something
of the dignitary in Walter's way
with people, cross bred as it is with the absent mind
of the professor and the sure hand of the gentleman
farmer (straight out of some lesser known
Frost poem). A soul emissary, then, who
at present—as we pass up through
the burgeoning pines, along a New England
stone wall—is asking about my father,
recently dead, about how it has been
dealing with the aftermath and all
the troubled souls that end up at the door
of the dead poet's house uninvited.
He seems to understand: brother, father,
teacher—yes, even son. He's that good
at listening. And listening, too, for some echo
out of the forest, some crow flap to awaken
an answer (in me?). He just nods. We keep walking
and as we go forward, me conjuring my
love for my father, I feel some hidden part
dislodge, take wing, fly up
to join the crow in the late afternoon haze—
my body moving onward with Walter, as light
as cumulus clouds passing soundlessly over water.

COMING TO FLOOD

The fields, just the other day lost to water,
have emerged saturated in green, decked-out

in the new day, the only sign of the flood's
accidental profusion a few skewed mud tracks,

branches wedged into a fence, a propane tank
placed daintily in the fork of a tree, and I,

groggy from lack of coffee, drive into a bank
of fog, hung like a sheet, cloaking everything

but the stutter of broken yellow center line,
for a vast moment in no place, nowhere

suspended, until the fields reappear, now
a ceiling for the upside-down sky, another

kind of flood, one more border
crossing. When I first spied the river

elbowing out of its banks, brown as stew,
unruly, threatening to convert cow fields,

I wanted you beside me, unfastened.
You'd want to get close to the raging,

to undress in solidarity, throwing clothing
into the great convergence. At flood peak,

I took the dog along our normal route,
down through the green locks of the public course,

an impromptu body of muddy water
where fairway used to be. We came to the edge

of the new current, old road no longer a direction,
and sniffed at the air. The river had let drop

its dress, a tumble of rustling fabric over its banks;
those who lived at its feet were getting nervous.

When a friend had me over to her house, a retreat
perfect in its components, a living room made

for making love in, all slanting sun and throw pillows,
she joked: "We'll be airlifted out of here."

She was right, almost, for by midnight she'd fled,
and in the morning the flood, restless

neighborhood kid, had ransacked her house,
leaving signs everywhere of its ruinous company.

FALL

A little circus makes its way
into any ordinary day,
slipping in with pickpocket hand.

Just today, we rounded the bend
to find two goats in collars
out for a riverside stroll,

their sweet, alien eyes mooning
out at everything. Back home,
chasing after my unleashed dog,

I stepped into a pile of leaves
(the hidden slope beneath letting
go) and pratfell down a knoll

of blackout mulch. Coming up
in a three-point stance. Before me:
the neighbor's dog atremble,

snarling at last gasp of lead. Even
now, up at my desk, the sun
shines a spot on the bookshelf,

turning my dog-eared paperbacks
into illuminated manuscripts,
and a trapdoor opens in my head.

PRAYER

When Sonny Rollins walked onto that bridge
to play his saxophone to the wind
he was stepping off the stage
and into the woodshed.
It wasn't a failure of nerve, of course,
nor was it only a deepening
of his craft. He was breaking
a voice apart
and refashioning it.
He was undressing his muse.

That's what I want now:
less stage, more bridge
(the wind steady and relentless)
and room to go about
the private business of becoming—
nothing more, not a single iota less—
who I am meant to be.

And if that's asking
too much, then allow me to rest
a moment, and when I wake
let me be refreshed.

WE GENEROUS

> *What does a man say, when he doesn't want to   erupt,*
> *but still wants to act like a man?*
> —A. Van Jordan, "Notes of a Southpaw"

Long past midnight; hard rain.
Somewhere twenty, thirty blocks

west the downtown Chicago grid,
in a neighborhood taxis don't come to

or stop in this late: in search
of the sublime, gawkers

at the *Velvet Lounge*, "soul hole"
box-cared alongside *Fitzsi's Famous*,

fresh out of two epic sets—
avant-garde jazz played wildly

but seriously by a cabal of young lions
gathered round their greybeard leader—

saturated down through our jackets,
laughing about it, falling

into a kind of sadsack parody
of a gang's strut. I want to say

"a bunch of white guys," but
that's not exactly true, not really

the point: comrades, then, ecstatic
encounterers of rain-slicked streets,

eager to inhabit this one particular
moment whole-souled and sad.

⌘

Hip enough to recognize, when
the bartender puts him on, Tatum—

his slalom runs and storm-pitch
arpeggios a kind of sped-up Bud Powell

(funny how influence runs backward
to the avid listener's ear before

catching on a quirk of period detail
and starting up again, face forward)—

hip enough to order drinks wiped clean
of class, to clap in the right places,

though with these guys it ain't easy
anticipating the step-back pause

inside the soloist's circular breathing.
Trying not to look like a fool.

⌘

The young baritone dips and prances,
spraying avuncular chords

from an ancient hockshop horn, propping
his leg on the stage like a trap-door hinge.

One song bleeding into the next;
drummers switching mid-bridge.

A flute player sits in, the only white guy
on stage, bald, and screams

into the cup of his flute,
the bass pulsing triple time, clanging

like at a railroad crossing, horns
coming together in cacophony.

After five minutes of an extended riff
on the absence of beauty (an old sweater

turned inside-out, straight-jacketed)
I get the hell out. The street

album-cover empty. Drizzle.
I yearn for something to hold

between my fingers. Something
to breathe my sweet blue self back into.

Sabotage always blows things up
answering its own urgent question.

⌘

Remember that Thai place on Franklin?
I keep seeing us step out into that L.A. oven

to discover Peter's little VW
book-ended by cop-cars. "Bad omen,"

I say. "I choose to see it as they're looking
out for my best interest." Which I assume

he means spiritually, a black man's
sarcastic prayer against indirect malice.

You read a poem that night
about being called *nigger* by a white man

with a bar stool for a handshake.
How at great cost you beat him

into submission. The lone black man
in the audience comes up, shakes

your hand. Says he can relate.
Later, in Leimert Park, Peter leans over

to say something about vertigo overtaking you
when you're out of your element.

⌘

The lunch joint's got Elvis on the radio.
I keep drifting, following the birds'

choppy path through the sun-gutted windows,
adding turns and banks I can't quite see:

they seem first to fly through a fence
then morph into schooling fish shivering

in a landscape of blue. There's this video
you stayed up late for, ringing your mind's

backdoor bell. In it, some white collar guy
dreams he finds God crouched in a dingy closet

in a building at the heart of a city on fire—
Dresden or Los Angeles—and though

He has the head of a lion, God
is scared. The man must take his hand

to reassure Him. You give me this look
I can't read but falls heavy onto the counter

into the bowl of your hands. Let me guess:
you're trying, but in this moment failing,

to inhabit the world in a manner
akin to prayer. Don't you know

this country has always enjoyed a minstrel show?
Even better when the blackface is invisible

and the man shimmying onstage
isn't that hit parade of soul

but some country white boy with hips like a girl's
and soulful eyes your mama'd melt for.

⌘

We're lucky to catch a train
before the station closes down:

the rain refuses to stop playing.
This kid in a Bulls jersey, no more

than fourteen, starts right in.
Sneering "You Irish?" Then:

"You white folks are crazy."
Right after that, with a comic's

timing: "Get me a fucking job!"
There's anger there but bluff

mostly what I see. Too tired
to harass him back or move

to another seat. Can only smile.
(Maybe our fight is not to *be* awake—

we're resurrected all the time
by fire—but to stay that way.)

The familiar rocking
of the subway carries us

into the next station of night.
It's a calm resignation cities bring.

Our faces show our fatigue.
And our happiness.

⌘

What is it about this country that makes
it hard even to be friends?

Riding down the 10 that night
in a friend's low-slung sports car,

Coltrane in place of the rap
basted on the way out, the lights

of the Inland Valley sequin
the night. I start to say

"I like my anger beautiful"
but know it's a matter up for discussion

and so let the night's bad breath
wash us raw. The freeway crowded

at midnight; I think you are falling asleep.
You're just taking in Trane through your pores.

⌘

Man, that baritone!
How he grabbed hold of

that funky R&B riff
and rode its freight-train circuit

(compact body only
slightly taller than the horn)

swinging lovingly
in its current.

We rocked a little, too,
on the edge of our chairs

and the woman behind the bar
allowed the rhythm

to carry her into her
habitual chores

as the man
on his way to the john

fell easily
into its rutted sway.

⌘

When did conversation swerve
to the morning's headline slap?

*Policeman Guns Down
Unarmed Black Man.*

"Same old shit," you mutter.
I think: who's to say some madman

wouldn't take us out? Carnival
cut-outs knocked down

blam blam blam
with three twitchy trigger pulls.

Memory's clumsy. So much left out,
so many subtle add-ins. Did I

really spy a billboard
(Marvin Gaye's "What's Going On"

dancing in my head) that,
for a second, read "We Generous"

before blinking and seeing
what the words actually said?

Maybe this is all just
my white man's guilt urge

to go down in flames.
Sometimes it's all I've got.

⌘

There's a story about Art Pepper.
Fresh out of jail, he's between everything—

gigs, fixes, horns. Diane arranges a gig,
not telling Art, so he wakes to the news

he's playing with Miles' rhythm section:
Philly Joe, Garland, Chambers on bass.

He's afraid, of course, hasn't touched his horn
in months, cork stuck in its neck and taped

in place. Mad at Diane. In awe.
"They've been playing with Miles. They're masters."

He'd been goofing, fixing big before.
Forgets every song in the book.

So Gentleman Red says: "I know a nice tune.
Do you know this?" And Art plays it beautiful,

chasing after the melody of "You'd Be So Nice
to Come Home to." Lets Red call the songs

rest of the way. "What should I do at the end?"
"Just do a little tag kind of thing."

And Art does. They get eight songs
on tape. After, she gives him a look

that asks, "Happy?" Yeah, he's happy.
Worried, too, he's not played well enough.

And proud, bragging up his genius
like a cocky boy. The night he falls back

into dope, six months clean,
he tells Diane, "You have to know

someone loves you. When you do,
everything is easier."

⌘

Something about that crowded table
of young musicians—in between

sets, cordoned off by invisible rope.
Is it they didn't look over once

all night? That's not it.
Any circle worth its form curls inward,

a spring about to unfurl in a snap.
Too loud to talk, anyway.

Were we two brotherhoods meeting
for a night? Can you call such proximity

a meeting? The way a man and a woman
share a smoke outside a club

not knowing what to do
with the plentitude of loneliness

except refrain from offering
some of its sweetness to one another.

⌘

The storm has swept through, leaving
the streets wet. Schoolgirls trundling by

in full dress. Beat, on our way
for coffee, hangovers pulled down

like soggy hats, bullshitting,
stretching out the walk

through the rain into epic length,
when a crew of girl scouts

accosts us, hawking their wares,
like the street gypsies in Florence

flashing cardboard up at tourist faces,
bringing hands away from pockets,

cutting into your body with razor fingers.
A scout steps in our path and shouts,

"You know you want it!" We laugh. We do.
We do and we don't. As if we had a choice.

WE FALL INTO SHAPES
AND BREATHE DEEPLY

A young musician asleep on a train,
already famous, or soon will be.
You strain to see, don't want to be rude.
Face open, innocent, he sleeps
like a boy, full weight on his elbows;
and though there is no way
to know this, you are sure
he has no change in his pockets—
old bandmates or devotees
picking him up at the station
to deliver him to his next meal.
You should keep moving,
not block the aisle, but you want
the light to fall like this always
in the dark rooms of trains.
To slant across the expanse
of his face, eyes closed as if
by tender fingers, mouth
slightly open. You want to place
a coin on his lips in homage
to all the music that will blossom there.

—after Milt Hinton

WOLF WITH YOU

Life's funny
in that hat flying off
in the wind sort of way

the way dreams are funny
when they drop a wolf in
to tug at a sleeve

and all you want
is to get over the fence
and be gone;

or when the one who
first time you saw her
was the mad lady on the corner

wailing outside your father's funeral,
a sort of wolf tugging
at the sleeve of decorum,

this raving woman
with the spurned-lover eyes,
somehow the surrogate

who fills the role
the other one refrained from
when she thought she got

cut out, not willing
to take her sack of woe
and join the rest of us

in the long line
of the empty-handed;
the mad lady the one

who steps off the curb
of the inappropriate,
demonstrating the uncanny

way to get over the fence
and take the dream
wolf with you.

GOT THOSE CARY GRANT BLUES AGAIN

Even Cary Grant wanted to be Cary Grant.
We all know that. Still, ain't it hard
when the old daydream machine
breaks down on the side of the road

and you're left to change your body's tire?
A scraped-knuckles day. The pockets
of your coat eaten through by the dog
and coins scattered all down the river.

Even Cary Grant needs a vacation
from the cruise boat of his image. *Let me off,*
he hisses, as he bandy-legs the plank
and runs down the ragged Medallion. *Get me*

the hell out of here. Cough of smoke
like a balloon tied to the antenna. *And fast.*
Where do you go, though? The bazaar?
It's full of tatterdemalions and bandicoots,

downtrodden women eyeballing
your diamond links. The cafes thronged
with paperback Sartres and terrorists
who've lost track of the maps of their souls.

Gurdjieff sat there once, wallowing in secret
histories, waiting for Ouspensky
to write it down on the oragami'd napkin.
Waiter, check please. And Durell's Darley

wandered these same streets, chasing
down the ghost-steps of Justine, that sacred
whore of his colonial mind. Nothing's new.
All the trade routes have been sewn. The electric

line of college-student desire has lost
its sparkle: only a picketpocket's route
to hollowed-out monuments. Even
a trek along sacred ridgeline

no longer rings true
in high mountain air. Even Cary Grant
wanted to be free of his name.
I'm here, you shout, *I'm fucking here.*

BUYING WINE

When we were boys, we had a choice: stay in the car or else
follow him into Wine Mart, that cavernous retail barn,

down aisle after aisle—California reds to Australian blends
to French dessert wines—past bins loaded like bat racks

with bottles, each with its own heraldic tag, its licked coat
of arms, trailing after our father as he pushed the ever-filling cart,

bent forward in concentration, one hand in mouth stroking
his unkempt mustache, the other lofting up bottles like fruit

then setting them down, weighing the store of data in his brain
against the cost, the year, the cut of meat he'd select at the butcher's:

a lamb chop, say, if this Umbrian red had enough body to marry,
to dance on its legs in the bell of the night; or some scallops maybe,

those languid hearts of the sea, a poet's dozen in a baggy,
and a Pinot Grigio light enough not to disturb their salty murmur.

Often, we'd stay in the car until we'd used up the radio
and our dwindling capacity to believe our father

might actually "Just be back," then break free, releasing
our seatbelts, drifting to the edges of the parking lot like horses

loosed in a field following the sun's endgame of shade; sometimes
I'd peer into the front window, breath fogging the sale signs,

catching snippets of my father's profile appearing and disappearing
behind the tall cardboard stacks. Once I slipped back into the store,

wandering the aisles, master of my own cart, loading it to bursting for the dream party I was going to throw. But mostly, like now,

as I search for the perfect $12 bottle, I'd shuffle along, dancing bear behind circus master, and wait for my father to pronounce, tall

in his basketball body, wine bottles like babies in his hands, "Aha!"

ROUND THE BEND

Not all veils obscure.

Just this morning
at a familiar bend
in the road to Warren Wilson
fog fills in the valley
like milk in a bowl, only
the topmost gable
of the barn visible. We are
stunned by the abundant nothingness:
brought abruptly into ourselves
then boomeranged
back into the day
through spectator eyes.

I drop you off.
Ursula lays in a contented
heap in the backseat.
Something good on the deck.
And when I pass the farm
again, at the turn,
this time emerging
from out of a tunnel of fog,
I cast a glance over
my shoulder. Milk in a bowl?
What was I thinking?
A fierce dragon
festooned in rivers of ashen silk
roars up through the light,
consuming the barn
as flame feeds on heat.

Then again,
at the top of the hill,
about to turn onto Old Farm School,
a bed sheet luffs
in the rearview mirror.
And for a moment
I watch it float
in the sun,
a muted music
of undulation

and then I round the bend.

THE NIGHT BEFORE AVERY ARRIVES

We've finally drifted off to sleep, our dreams
rabbit-running through an open field,
eager to drive down three hours to fetch you,
then back up the same stretch of highway home.

The bread bowl of neighborhood brims
with noisy dark; no one is out. Old friends
talk on the phone; our parents drift
in easy talk, old stories brought out again.

Your birth mother is out of range, dyeing
her hair in the sink of a motel room;
one of your named fathers is tossing
in his bed, signing and resigning the form.

And you? Asleep, I hope, spilled of one code,
waiting for us to come and speak the new.

WHAT LOVE IS

You could tell he was a Marsalis
brother, even sitting in the back:
he had that muddy river lilt

in his voice, the bristling intellect
and the irrepressible need to teach
the storied history of African-

American classical music. Jazz
was in his blood as legacy.
The *Funky Butt* was jammed, only this

back table free, whiskeys on the way.
A Basie number, Monk. The band
tight, Delfeayo's trombone aflame

from the opening chorus. I even
didn't mind that nearby tables
were more chatter than rapt attention,

or that our waitress took her time.
For Delfeayo was holding forth
on the subject of "cuttin'," that

fraternal pissing contest where raw-
boned skill and bravado run loose
to fight for the night's supremacy.

When the trumpet got introduced,
he looked over at Marsalis, a little
reticent to step into the ring.

Who could blame him? Delfeayo was all
over the bone: so low in the register
your feet could feel it; so high

he was bumping the night's rafters.
And not just range. He donned all the hats
of virtuosity in rapid succession

and swung like crazy, too. The trumpeter
was game, following behind
like a younger brother, tossing up

the bell of his horn, blatting out wild
roundhouse notes. But he was going
down. And when he managed a high

C, and held it, it came from his waist:
he'd been cut off at the legs. We
nearly jumped out of our seats, like

at some cellar cock fight.
At the break, heading for the john,
I spied a couple groping

in the dark hall; the woman pushing
the man up against a wall, kissing
him hard; his hand cupping her ass.

And when the waitress set down our drinks,
her breasts dropping like ripe peaches,
a cowgirl tattoo dancing on her arm,

I just about burst into happiness—
for being among friends,
for loving my wife, who

I knew, was at home
in front of the fire, dog asleep
at her feet—and raised a silent

toast to the night unfolding:
to soulful music and to the grace-
ful glance of good luck's passing.

Later, when Delfeayo played
the loveliest solo on "You Don't Know
What Love Is" I ever heard

(heroin slow, each note laid out
like an early morning baker
sets out a rack of bread loaves)

the place got church quiet, drinks
clinking as we listened in
on a one-way lover's plea

into the grimy pay phone of the blues.
Before we left, the couple returned,
the guy's shirt back basted

with brick dust and sweat. I shook
Marsalis' hand on the way out
in that tentative way blacks and whites

do, half soul shake, half *how you do?*
and told him what I thought of his solo.
He gave me a look I couldn't read,

that I'd like to think registered surprise.
What do I know? Out on the street,
on the walk back to the hotel,

past a broken-bottled Congo Square,
the four of us picked our way
through the drunks—city still

bustling past midnight, sidewalks
slick from a streetsweep of rain—
jabbering about the prize fight

of a set, and I tried to
tell my friend something
of the feeling that had taken

hold of me, stumbling over
the words like a greenhorn
sitting in. He listened, rapt, happy,

filling in the last gap
of my music with a huge *whoop*
and then, steps later, *Wow!*

Wow! and we crossed over
onto Canal, heads bent in reverie
for all the night had offered up in its swell.

www.ingramcontent.com/pod-product-compliance
Lightning Source LLC
Chambersburg PA
CBHW022346040426
42449CB00006B/740